INVASIVE SPECIES

PURPLE LOOSESTRIFE

by Alicia Z. Klepeis

Ideas for Parents and Teachers

Pogo Books let children practice reading informational text while introducing them to nonfiction features such as headings, labels, sidebars, maps, and diagrams, as well as a table of contents, glossary, and index.

Carefully leveled text with a strong photo match offers early fluent readers the support they need to succeed.

Before Reading

- "Walk" through the book and point out the various nonfiction features. Ask the student what purpose each feature serves.
- Look at the glossary together. Read and discuss the words.

Read the Book

- Have the child read the book independently.
- Invite him or her to list questions that arise from reading.

After Reading

- Discuss the child's questions. Talk about how he or she might find answers to those questions.
- Prompt the child to think more. Ask: Purple loosestrife spreads fast. It can clog waterways and crowd out native plants. Can you name any other plants that do this?

Pogo Books are published by Jump!
5357 Penn Avenue South
Minneapolis, MN 55419
www.jumplibrary.com

Library of Congress Cataloging-in-Publication Data

Names: Klepeis, Alicia, 1971- author.
Title: Purple loosestrife / by Alicia Z. Klepeis.
Description: Minneapolis, MN: Jump!, Inc., [2023]
Series: Invasive species | Includes index.
Audience: Ages 7-10
Identifiers: LCCN 2022031798 (print)
LCCN 2022031799 (ebook)
ISBN 9798885241168 (hardcover)
ISBN 9798885241175 (paperback)
ISBN 9798885241182 (ebook)
Subjects: LCSH: Purple loosestrife–Juvenile literature. Invasive plants–Juvenile literature.
Classification: LCC QK495.L9 K54 2023 (print)
LCC QK495.L9 (ebook)
DDC 583/.73–dc23/eng/20220721
LC record available at https://lccn.loc.gov/2022031798
LC ebook record available at https://lccn.loc.gov/2022031799

Editor: Eliza Leahy
Designer: Emma Bersie

Photo Credits: Shutterstock, cover; Marccophoto/iStock, 1; spline_x/Shutterstock, 3; Ivonne Wierink/Dreamstime, 4; Wirestock Creators/Shutterstock, 5; Ole Schoener/Shutterstock, 6-7; Kristjan Veski/Shutterstock, 8-9tl; Tt/Dreamstime, 8-9tr; Rini Kools/Shutterstock, 8-9bl; blickwinkel/Alamy, 8-9br; Nahhana/Shutterstock, 10; Ruud Morijn Photographer/Shutterstock, 11; Peter Turner Photography/Shutterstock, 12-13; Tatyana Mut/Shutterstock, 14-15; mauritius images GmbH/Alamy, 16-17; Tom Dodge/The Columbus Dispatch/AP Images, 18; agefotostock/Alamy, 19; Lipatova Maryna/Shutterstock, 20-21; Kazakov Maksim/Shutterstock, 23.

Printed in the United States of America at Corporate Graphics in North Mankato, Minnesota.

TABLE OF CONTENTS

CHAPTER 1

MILLIONS OF SEEDS

What plant has purple-pink flowers and produces millions of seeds? It is purple loosestrife! This plant can be six feet (1.8 meters) tall. It has narrow green leaves.

Its flowers draw in butterflies and bees. These insects **pollinate** the plant. Then it grows fruit and seeds.

Purple loosestrife is **native** to Europe, Asia, Australia, and northern Africa. In these areas, it grows in streams, **wetlands**, woodlands, and **fen meadows**. It is an **invasive species** in the United States and Canada.

TAKE A LOOK!

Where is purple loosestrife in the United States and Canada? Take a look!

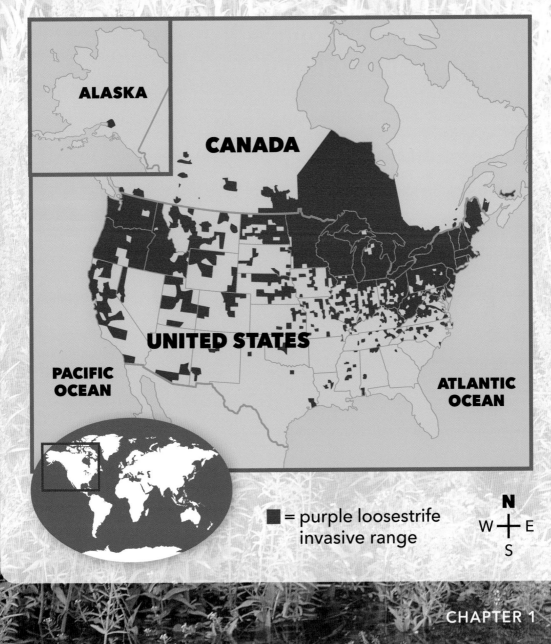

ALASKA

CANADA

UNITED STATES

PACIFIC OCEAN

ATLANTIC OCEAN

■ = purple loosestrife invasive range

N W E S

Purple loosestrife **adapts** well. This helps it spread. It can live in sun or shade. It can grow in different kinds of soil. It grows in many **habitats**. These include meadows and wetlands. It can even grow in standing water!

CHAPTER 2

WATCH OUT, WETLANDS!

Purple loosestrife came to North America in the early 1800s. How? This plant has tiny seeds. They are the size of grains of sand! They travel easily by water and wind. They likely came from Europe in the **ballast water** of ships.

seed pod

Over time, they spread by rivers and streams. **Aquatic** animals like muskrats, ducks, and swans also move the seeds. The seeds get stuck in their fur or feathers.

People accidentally spread this plant. How? Seeds get stuck in mud. Mud attaches to shoes and vehicles. The seeds travel to new areas. New plants grow.

In the past, many people planted these plants in their gardens. They thought it looked pretty. Others used it as medicine. Some **nurseries** still sell it.

DID YOU KNOW?

One purple loosestrife plant produces more than 2 million seeds each year.

Purple loosestrife grows fast. It has thick roots. They grow underground **runners**. These form a **dense** mat. It crowds out native plants. It takes food and shelter away from native wildlife.

DID YOU KNOW?

A purple loosestrife plant can live for more than 20 years.

purple
loosestrife

This plant's leaves and roots can **clog** waterways. This slows the flow of water. It can stop boats from traveling through. This makes it harder for people to fish and hunt.

CHAPTER 3

· ·

BEETLES TO THE RESCUE

Scientists want to learn more about purple loosestrife. They **track** it. They study how mowing affects its spread. Why? Mowing breaks up the plants. The pieces form roots. These grow into new plants.

black-margined loosestrife beetle

Scientists release beetles from Europe. The beetles eat purple loosestrife. This helps stop it from growing and spreading.

You can help stop the spread, too. How? Do not plant purple loosestrife. If you see it growing near you, cut off the flowers. Put them in a bag and throw them away. This prevents its seeds from spreading. It helps native plants and animals!

ACTIVITIES & TOOLS

WETLANDS NEAR YOU

The spread of purple loosestrife harms North American wetlands. Discover wetland plants and animals in your area with this fun activity!

What You Need:
- colored pencils, crayons, or markers
- clipboard
- white construction paper or other drawing paper
- plant identification guide or phone with a free plant identification app
- pencil
- notebook

1. Visit a wetland in your area with an adult. It could be a swamp, an area near a stream, or any other slightly marshy area. Bring a clipboard and drawing supplies.

2. Sketch the wetland in as much detail as you can. Be sure to draw some of the plants that grow in it.

3. Use a plant identification guide or app to learn what plants are in the wetland. Make a list of the ones you find.

4. Did you see any purple loosestrife? What are some similarities between the plants you saw and purple loosestrife? What are some differences?

adapts: Changes to fit a new situation.

aquatic: Living in or often found in water.

ballast water: Water that is held in tanks and cargo holds of ships to keep the ships stable.

clog: To fill up or block something.

dense: Crowded or thick.

fen meadows: Low, marshy areas of land that are often flooded.

habitats: The places where animals or plants are usually found.

invasive species: Any kind of living organism that is not native to a specific area.

native: Growing or living naturally in a particular area of the world.

nurseries: Places that sell trees, plants, and seeds.

pollinate: To take pollen from the male part of a flower and put it on the female part of a flower so the plant can reproduce.

runners: Thin, creeping stems that grow out from a plant's base.

track: To follow and try to find a plant by looking for marks or traces of it.

wetlands: Areas of land where there is a lot of moisture in the soil.

INDEX

TO LEARN MORE

Finding more information is as easy as 1, 2, 3.

❶ Go to www.factsurfer.com

❷ Enter "purpleloosestrife" into the search box.

❸ Choose your book to see a list of websites.

FACT SURFER